CITY ON THE GO

Toronto

RENNAY CRAATS

Published by Weigl Educational Publishers Limited
6325 – 10 Street SE
Calgary, Alberta, Canada
T2H 2Z9
Web site: http://www.weigl.com
Copyright © 2002 WEIGL EDUCATIONAL PUBLISHERS LIMITED

National Library of Canada Cataloguing in Publication Data
Craats, Rennay, 1973
  Toronto

  (Canadian Cities)
  Includes Index
  ISBN 1-896990-65-7

  1. Toronto (Ont)--Juvenile literature. I. Title. II. Series:
Canadian Cities (Calgary, Alta)
FC3097.33.C72 2001   j971.3'541   C2001-910656-4
F1059.5.T684C72 2001

Printed and bound in Canada
1 2 3 4 5 6 7 8 9 0   05 04 03 02 01

Project Coordinator
Jill Foran
Design
Warren Clark
Cover Design
Terry Paulhus
Layout
Lucinda Cage
Photo Research
Tina Schwartzenberger

We acknowledge the
financial support of
the Government of
Canada through the
Book Publishing
Industry Development
Program (BPIDP) for
our publishing activities.

Photograph Credits

Every reasonable effort has been made to trace ownership and to obtain permission to reprint copyright material. The publishers would be pleased to have any errors or omissions brought to their attention so that they may be corrected in subsequent printings.

Cover: Lampo Communications; Inside Cover: Lampo Communications; Greg Abel Photography: page 21T; Barrett & MacKay: page 16; Simon Bell/Toronto Zoo: page 20B; Chris Cheadle: page 23B; Peter Colleran/Surph Visual Communications: page 24T; Creative Stock Group: pages 4MR, 4B, 13BL, 13BR, 14TR, 15M, 25B, 28R; Epitome Pictures: page 29B; Government of Ontario Art Collection, Thomas Moore: page 6B; Hockey Hall of Fame: page 25T; Elaine Kilburn/Casa Loma: page 26; Lampo Communications: pages 3TL, 5M, 5BR, 23T, 27T; Legislative Assembly of Ontario: page 27B; MZTV Museum: page 22B; National Archives Canada: pages 6M (PA060734), 7T (C24937), 7B (C4782), 8M (PA042357), 8B (PA138682), 10T (C052029), 10B (PA053384), 30MR (C24937); O&Y Properties: page 28L; Paramount Canada's Wonderland: page 24B; Photofest: page 11T; PhotoSpin: pages 3B, 20M; Royal Ontario Museum: pages 3TR, 22T; Tina Schwartzenberger: page 14M; Second City Television (SCTV): page 12T; Skydome: pages 21B, 29T; Toronto City Hall: page 11B; Toronto Department of Economics: page 17T, 17B; Toronto GO-Transit: page 18T, 30B; Toronto Police Service: page 8TR; Toronto Special Events: page 12B, 13T; Toronto Transit Commission: page 18M; Toronto Transit Commission Archives: pages 9M, 9B; University of Toronto: page 19; Ignac Zajac: page 15B.

Contents

Introduction

Toronto is the capital of Ontario and the heart of Canada's industrial and financial region. It lies near the border of Canada and the United States, on the northwestern shores of Lake Ontario. It is also on the Saint Lawrence Seaway. This location makes it an ideal place for business and transportation.

Canada

0   500 km

Toronto

Getting There

Getting to Toronto is easy. Lester B. Pearson International Airport hosts a large number of flights every day—it is the busiest airport in Canada. Trains also arrive from several locations, and drivers can take one of the many highways that connect to the city.

At a Glance

Climate

Toronto's climate is influenced by its location. Lake Ontario helps moderate the weather. Winds from the lake make the winters a bit warmer and the summers a bit cooler. The winds also raise the city's humidity level.

Toronto's temperature in the winter is often below freezing, ranging from –1° Celsius to –8°C. In the summer, temperatures range from 18°C to 27°C.

Area & Population

Toronto covers a large area. It is made up of many regions that came together on January 1, 1998 to create the huge City of Toronto. These areas included North York, York, Etobicoke, Scarborough, and the **borough** of East York. Metropolitan Toronto spreads over 624 square kilometres. Greater Toronto, which includes the **suburban** areas of the city, is 5,868 sq km. Within this large area, the city is heavily populated. There are about 2.5 million people in metropolitan Toronto, but the city's surrounding areas boost the population to about 4.7 million.

The Waterfront

Water has always been important in Toronto. The waterfront is a place of great activity. The Harbourfront Centre is the hub of the area. This facility hosts performing arts as well as many residential, commercial, and retail developments. Torontonians can enjoy the parks and the hiking or cycling trails near the waterfront. Also, marinas in the area dock ships and pleasure boats.

Interesting Statistics

1. Toronto is less than 150 km from the New York State border.

2. Toronto has more than ninety ethnic groups, and about one hundred languages are spoken in the city.

3. Foreign-born residents make up about 50 percent of Toronto's population.

4. Five times in a row, the United Nations voted Toronto the most cosmopolitan and multicultural city in the world.

5. Toronto's total area is larger than any other city in Canada.

The Past

Early Settlement

Iroquois were the first to settle in the area now known as Toronto. They established a settlement along the east bank of the Humber River. Other Native Peoples frequently passed through the Toronto area while travelling between Lake Ontario and Lake Huron.

European explorers began to pass through the region in the seventeenth century. In 1750, the French created a fur-trading post, a fort, and a mission in the area that is now Toronto. During a battle with the British in 1759, the French decided to burn the fort to the ground rather than allow it to be taken over. By 1763, Britain controlled the area, but many of the French settlers remained there. After Britain lost the **American Revolution**, British citizens living in the United States decided to leave their homes and settle in Canada. A large portion of these 40,000 **Loyalists** resettled in what would become Ontario.

The first permanent British settlement in Toronto was built in 1793. This settlement was called York, after the son of King George III. The old French fort was rebuilt and became Fort Toronto. People settled around it, establishing a city.

The settlement of York soon grew to have a government and a system of roadways.

Key Events

1775–1783
British settlers, called Loyalists, flee the United States and settle in Canada.

1793
John Graves Simcoe selects the Toronto area as the first permanent capital of Upper Canada, naming it York.

1812–1814
The United States declares war on Britain and invades Canada. York's buildings are pillaged and destroyed.

The Government

York was destroyed during the War of 1812. It was rebuilt as soon as the war was over. From 1815 to 1841, the city hosted Upper Canada's government. It was run by the Family Compact, which made decisions based on its own interests. People became angry at this, and they looked to a Scotsman named William Lyon Mackenzie to change the system. He was elected mayor of the renamed city of Toronto in 1834.

Mackenzie worked to change the system of government, but the Compact destroyed Mackenzie's newspaper presses and tried to stop him. In 1837, Mackenzie and his supporters fought back. About 800 people marched down Yonge Street to demand control of Toronto. Although the Compact defeated them in that confrontation, the British government began to pay attention to the city's unrest. The Family Compact was **dismantled**, and Mackenzie's democracy soon became a

William Lyon Mackenzie was a prominent journalist and politician before he was elected mayor of Toronto in 1834.

reality. By 1848, a **representative government** was in place.

Over the years, the city grew. Neighbouring townships and cities established themselves as individual municipalities. In 1954, thirteen municipalities came together to create six regions, all controlled by Metropolitan Toronto. Then, on January 1, 1998, these municipalities were officially joined together again to create a single municipality called the City of Toronto. It provides its citizens with fundamental services including policing, public transit, social services, and garbage disposal.

1834
York becomes a city and is renamed Toronto.
1837
William Lyon Mackenzie's rebellion fails.

1840
Act of Union brings together Upper Canada (Ontario) and Lower Canada (Quebec) to form The United Province of Canada.

Law and Order

Toronto's police department was established in 1834. It was run by five full-time constables who earned $150 each year. Fourteen other special constables helped out, but they were not paid for their contribution. These men were in charge of maintaining peace in a city that had grown to more than 9,000 people.

The constables were given the tough job of catching shopkeepers who threw their garbage onto Yonge Street. Constables were also asked to prevent **bootlegging**, and to stop people from speeding down the streets on their horses, or from riding their horses on the sidewalks. Police officers enforced the rules against driving cattle through city streets, and ensured that citizens were respecting the **Sabbath**—people were expected to rest and worship, not work, on Sundays.

As Toronto grew, so did the police force. It has expanded incredibly from

The Toronto Police Service is the second oldest police service in Canada. Toronto's police officers now have the use of about 1,160 cars, 129 motorcycles, 25 horses, 15 dogs, and 18 boats to ensure order is maintained.

its small beginnings. By 1998, the police force had 4,904 uniformed police officers, 2,162 civilian employees, and 238 police **auxiliary** officers.

Key Events

1834
The police department is established.
1835
Part of Toronto's Yonge Street is paved.

1837 Police officers are issued uniforms.
1853 The first Canadian railway steam engine is built and operated in Toronto.

Transportation

In 1849, the Williams Omnibus Bus Line became the first public transportation company in Toronto. It drove passengers along Yonge Street in horse-drawn coaches. By 1861, the city had its first street rail franchise in place. However, Torontonians still had a tough time getting around. The difficulties in getting from one place to another in the city continued throughout the first half of the 1900s.

To ease some transportation problems, the city established the Toronto Transportation Commission (TTC) in 1921. The TTC made the nine fare systems in the city into one. It also added new routes to accommodate the expanding city.

The Williams Omnibus Bus Line was the first transportation company in Toronto.

Construction of the first section of Toronto's subway was completed in 1954. This section ran from Union Station to Eglinton Avenue.

Spy Camp

During World War II, the British created a spy school officially called Special Training School 103. It was nicknamed Camp X. The camp, built in 1941, lies just east of Toronto. The British wanted to find a location that was far from their enemies but close to their American allies. Ontario's location was perfect.

The school taught as many as 2,000 people from around the world between 1941 and 1944. What went on behind the walls of Camp X was kept a secret. The camp was protected by armed guards. Training stopped before the war was officially over. Camp X remained a military facility until the 1960s.

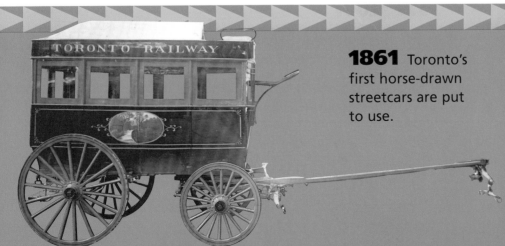

1861 Toronto's first horse-drawn streetcars are put to use.

1892 The first electric streetcar is operated and the last horse-drawn street car is taken off the streets two years later.

1949 Construction of Toronto's subway system begins.

Famous People

Mary Pickford
1893–1979

When she was 14 years old, Mary Pickford landed a lead role in a Broadway production. Two years later, she launched her movie career. Her sweetness and beauty made her popular, and her acting talent made her a superstar. Despite being Canadian, Mary was called "America's Sweetheart" and then "The World's Sweetheart." Throughout her career, she starred in many successful silent movies, including *The New York Hat* (1912), *Madame Butterfly* (1915), and *Daddy Long Legs* (1919). She starred in and produced many others, including *Rosita* (1923) and *My Best Girl* (1927). Mary was the first movie star to receive the incredible salary of $350,000 per movie. In 1919, she and a few fellow entertainers, including Charlie Chaplin and Douglas Fairbanks, formed their own studio called United Artists. Mary won an Academy Award for her role in *Coquette* in 1929.

Mary Pickford retired from movie-making in 1933.

Timothy Eaton
1834–1907

When Timothy Eaton was 20 years old, he moved from Ireland to Canada. He started his chain of department stores with

Timothy Eaton created a nationally successful retail giant.

a small dry-goods store in Toronto in 1869. His store was very different from any other store at that time. He set prices that were not negotiable. He also guaranteed the quality of the goods he sold. His dry-goods store expanded to include clothing, housewares, furniture, and, eventually, electronics. In 1883, he opened a large store on Yonge Street. This store had electric lights, elevators, washrooms, and even concerts. To accommodate shoppers in rural areas, Timothy offered mail-order catalogues. This made the T. Eaton Company stores a huge success.

Mike Myers
1963—

Mike Myers is a comedian who got his start in Toronto's Second City comedy troupe. For eight years, he performed **improv** to laughing audiences. In 1989, his dream came true when he joined the cast of *Saturday Night Live*. In his six years there, Mike created many memorable characters, including cable-show host Wayne,

Thanks to the great success of his movies, Mike is in demand in Hollywood.

and Dieter, the German host of *Sprockets*. He starred in such movies as *Wayne's World* and *So I Married an Axe Murderer* before he wrote and starred in *Austin Powers: International Man of Mystery*. This movie about a sixties spy in the nineties was a huge success. Mike released a sequel about Austin Powers to an equally appreciative audience.

Mel Lastman
1934—

After making millions of dollars in the appliances business, Mel Lastman

turned to public office to make his mark on the city. He has been in Toronto politics for decades. His energy and charisma have continually drawn voters to the polling booths to elect him back into office. Mel served a record twenty-five years as mayor of the former suburb of North York. In 1997, he won the right to head the **amalgamated** city of Toronto.

Mel Lastman is the longest-serving mayor of any major city in the world.

The Barenaked Ladies

Steven Page and Ed Robertson were friends in Toronto long before they formed their band, The Barenaked Ladies. It started out with the two of them performing in 1988. Then brothers Jim and Andy

Creegan and drummer Tyler Stewart joined the mix. The band recorded fun songs including "If I had a Million Dollars," "Be My Yoko Ono," and "Enid." They soon became favourites in Canada. They released their first album, *Gordon*, in 1992, and the record sold more

than 80,000 copies on the first day it was released. The band was named Best Group of the Year at the 1993 Juno Awards, and has enjoyed several nominations over the years. The Barenaked Ladies have released four other studio albums as well as a live recording.

Culture

The Arts

Toronto has long been a cultural centre for Ontario and Canada. The Group of Seven, who came together in Toronto, established a Canadian style of painting landscape in the 1920s. Other talented painters and artists have followed in their footsteps. Novelists, including Douglas Cooper and Margaret Atwood, also come from Toronto.

There are five major theatres in Toronto, including the Princess of Wales Theatre and the Ford Centre for the Performing Arts. Many smaller theatres in the city present lesser known productions. Theatre-lovers from all over North America travel to Toronto enjoy the great performances.

One of Toronto's most famous theatres is devoted to comedy. Created in 1973, The Second City was an offshoot of a successful comedy club in Chicago. The Toronto group was made up of such stars as Dan Aykroyd, Martin Short, John Candy, Andrea Martin, and Catherine O'Hara. Within a few years, The Second City Toronto became the country's number-one improvisational theatre. The cast brought its success to television with the hit show *SCTV*, and many went on to Hollywood stardom. The Toronto Symphony Orchestra, the National

The Second City Toronto is still a well-known and highly respected comedy club.

Ballet of Canada, and the Canadian Opera Company also provide Torontonians with world-renowned entertainment.

FESTIVALS

Every July, residents of Toronto enjoy the **Street Festival**. At this time, people celebrate the city, its culture, and the talented people who live there. There are four different festival sites located along Yonge Street. The festival presents everything from live music, to jugglers, to fire-eaters. More than 850,000 people enjoy the Street Festival every year.

Holiday Fun

Torontonians celebrate important holidays with great energy. Parades, festivals, and shows are often a part

Toronto's Winterfest has activities for everyone.

In September, the city hosts the **Toronto International Film Festival**. It is one of the best-attended film festivals in the world. Other festivals in Toronto include the **Kensington Karnival**, the **Ontario Renaissance Festival**, the **Chin Festival**, and the **Four Winds Kite Festival**.

of many popular holidays, including Canada Day. Every December, Toronto buzzes with activity. Festive light displays are found throughout the city. Ice skaters at Nathan Phillips Square twirl and glide around the Christmas tree and under strings of beautiful lights. The square is also the site of the annual ice-carving exhibition. Each entrant is given a block of ice weighing more than 135 kilograms and two days to chisel, chainsaw, and sculpt it. The resulting sculptures are amazing sights to see.

Torontonians enjoy other celebrations during the winter. Every February, the city holds Winterfest, a festival that runs for about three days. It entertains residents and visitors alike with many events and activities. Circus acts, famous performers, cultural exhibitions, and a midway are all part of the popular holiday festivities.

Every December, Nathan Phillips Square is lit up with about 100,000 Christmas lights.

All Kinds of Food

No matter what their tastes are, Torontonians can find just about every kind of food in their city. The population is made up of many different ethnic groups. These people brought their culture and cuisine with them when they moved to Toronto. As a result, restaurants showcasing Greek, Thai, Chinese, Italian, and Mexican food are found throughout the city. Chinatown is filled with stores offering Chinese foods and treats. Italian restaurants serving tasty pasta dishes and pizza can be found in nearly every neighbourhood.

Xoriatiki (Greek "Village" Salad)

Ingredients:

4 ripe tomatoes

1 cucumber

1 onion

1 green pepper

olives

capers

150 grams (1/3 lb) crumbled feta cheese

125 ml (1/2 cup) olive oil

oregano

salt

Slice the vegetables and mix together in a salad bowl. Top with the olives, capers, and oregano and cover with the crumbled feta cheese. Pour the olive oil evenly over the salad and season. This recipe serves six people.

Toronto's Chinatown is a great place to go for tasting new foods and browsing through interesting shops.

Greek Canadians have also preserved their culture and traditions in Toronto. There are many Greek restaurants in The Danforth, an area in Toronto. Greeks and non-Greeks alike flock to these restaurants for a taste of souvlaki, pilafi, or moussaka. Torontonians also enjoy food originating from other countries, as well as traditional French and British dishes.

Cultural Groups in Toronto

Over 50 percent of Toronto's population was born and raised in another country. After World War II, a huge number of immigrants arrived in Toronto. This changed the cultural makeup of the city so that it now has many ethnic neighbourhoods. Each of these neighbourhoods has a distinct personality and character. People of Chinese background make up more than 10 percent of metropolitan Toronto's population. The city's Chinatown offers a wide variety of Chinese pharmacies, theatres, restaurants, and shops.

Some reports say that there are as many Italians living in Toronto as there are in Florence, Italy. The city's Italian community established Little Italy, a place for Italians to meet, live, and sell traditional Italian foods and goods. Other large cultural groups in Toronto include Ukrainian, German, Portuguese, East Indian, Greek, and Polish. People from the Caribbean have also made Toronto their home. Every August, they host Caribana, a Caribbean costume and music festival.

Caribana is one of North America's largest cultural events. Over 1 million people attend the festival every year.

> ***Over 50 percent of Toronto's population was born and raised in another country.***

Toronto Slovak Dancers

Toronto has a strong Slovak community. The Toronto Slovak Dancers bring the cultural heritage of Slovakia to the rest of the city. Dances include "Horehronska Veselica," "Cerkany," "Perinarky Janosik," and "Veselica na Detve." Through these and other dances, the group brings Slovakian folk characters to life. By choosing music from all over Slovakia, the Toronto Slovak Dancers show the variety and beauty of Slovak traditions and stories. This talented dancing group has toured all over Canada and the United States. It has also toured Slovakia.

The Economy

Making Money

About 20 percent of Canada's income and 50 percent of Ontario's income is generated in Toronto. Many national companies have their headquarters in the city. In North America, only New York City and Chicago have more head offices.

Toronto is known for its financial businesses. These include the stock market, banks, insurance companies, and advertising and marketing firms. Publishing and printing are other major industries in Toronto.

Many of Toronto's major corporations are located on Bay Street. This street provides a snapshot of the city's financial success. Manufacturing, communications, entertainment, retail, and banking headquarters are all found on this downtown street. About 70 percent of the top fifty foreign-owned corporations in Canada operate on Bay Street. Many law firms and accounting firms have their offices on this street as well. The immense regional, national, and international business done on Bay Street every day has defined it as the centre of finance in Canada.

The many office buildings located on Bay Street are an indication of the city's enormous financial success.

Many national companies have their headquarters in Toronto.

Industries

Toronto is Canada's largest employment centre, providing one-sixth of the country's jobs. The city has a wide range of successful and competitive service and manufacturing industries. For example, Toronto-based companies such as Bombardier Aerospace and Spar Aerospace have helped make Canada's aerospace industry the fourth-largest in the world in terms of sales. Toronto is also the second-largest city for the manufacture of automobiles in North America.

The food and beverage industry is enormous in Toronto. Many of Canada's major food and beverage manufacturers

Many Toronto companies have been successful in producing advanced information technology.

are located there. The city is also home to a large pharmaceutical industry, with about 80 percent of Canada's generic drug manufacturers based there.

The media is also a significant contributor to Toronto's economy. The city has four major daily newspapers, four national television stations, and several radio stations. Moviemaking brings lots of money to the city as well. In fact, Toronto is considered to be North America's third-largest film and television production centre.

Toronto boasts an excellent information technology and telecommunications (IT&T) industry. The city is widely known as "Silicon Valley North" because it is home to over 2,200 IT&T companies, and produces many valuable computer-related goods. It also has the fourth-highest concentration of software companies in the world.

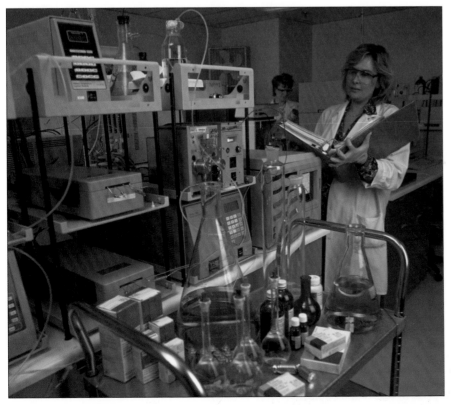

Important scientific research is conducted throughout the city every day.

Getting Around in Toronto

Toronto's transportation system is very efficient. With millions of people relying on it, it has to be. The Toronto Transit Commission (TTC) operates the buses, underground subways, and streetcars throughout the city. The streetcars run through the downtown section of the city and are a link to the city's past. To help people living in the suburban areas of Toronto, the GO transit system was created. Commuter trains and buses bring people to the metropolitan area from the surrounding regions.

Toronto's GO trains provide essential service for people who live in suburban areas. Streetcars carry passengers along many of the city's major routes.

A Touch of Britain

A local tour operator has brought a taste of Great Britain to Toronto's streets. Torontonians and tourists alike are welcome to hop onto the double-decker sightseeing buses. These buses are open at the top so riders can enjoy the Toronto sun while seeing the city. The company also offers tours in turn-of-the-century trolleys. People can visit attractions, shopping centres, and restaurants aboard these eye-catching tour buses. The tickets are good for twenty-four hours, so visitors can hop on and off as they wish throughout the day. The service promotes Toronto's many gardens, parks, and cultural sites.

Education

Toronto students have many post-secondary schools to choose from. The University of Toronto was established in 1827. The campus buildings stretch over blocks of downtown property, and the school accommodates more than 52,000 undergraduate and graduate students. Students can study engineering, business, law, education, medicine, and many other subjects at the University of Toronto. Ryerson Polytechnic University is located right in the heart of the city. It was founded in 1948. This school is known for excellent programs in such areas as interior design and journalism.

To the north of the city lies York University. It has been open to students since 1959. York is one of the leading research institutions in the country. Many research institutions, including the Centre for Applied Chemistry and the Institute for Space and Terrestrial Science, are located at York. Also, the university's law school is recognized around the world for its teaching and research in public policy. Toronto also has four community colleges, with campuses scattered throughout the city.

The University of Toronto is the largest university in Canada.

Sports and Recreation

Outdoor Fun

There is a great deal for nature lovers to do in Toronto. The city has around 100 parks and green spaces, and more than twenty provincial parks nearby. Hikers can tackle the trails, and those who prefer to relax can sit on the beaches. Fishing is another popular activity in and around Toronto.

The Beaches community in the city's east side is a great place to visit. The waterfront area offers sand, parks, and swimming. For a glimpse at incredible plants and flowers, Allan Gardens Conservatory is the place to go. The greenhouse is a humid hideaway full of tropical plants, prickly cacti, and colourful flowers. For those who prefer animals to plants, the Toronto Zoo has about 5,000 animals for visitors to learn more about. Hippopotamuses, orangutans, and giraffes entertain zoo patrons all year round. Other animal attractions in or around Toronto include the African Lion Safari, Marineland, Jungle Cat World, and the Niagara Parks Butterfly Conservatory.

At the Niagara Parks Butterfly Conservatory, visitors can walk among countless species of butterflies in a rain forest setting.

At the Toronto Zoo, visitors can learn more about all kinds of animals and plants through exciting exhibits and educational presentations.

Cheering on the Teams

Toronto is home to several impressive sports teams. The Toronto Maple Leafs are part of the National Hockey League. This team has excited the city's hockey fans since 1927. And fans have good reason to cheer. The team has brought the Stanley Cup home to Toronto eleven times since 1932.

The Toronto Blue Jays Major League Baseball team made history in 1992. They became the first non-American team to win the World Series. Then they repeated the victory the next year! The roster is full of talented players.

Basketball and football are also represented in the city. In 1995, the Toronto Raptors joined the National Basketball Association, becoming one of two Canadian teams in the league. The Toronto Argonauts compete in the

When they are in the city, the Toronto Maple Leafs play at the Air Canada Stadium.

Canadian Football League. The team won three Grey Cup championships in the 1990s, and have won fourteen since 1900.

The Skydome

The Skydome stadium was built in downtown Toronto in 1989. This arena was the first to boast a **retractable** roof. Within twenty minutes, the roof opens up and the playing field, along with most of the 50,000 seats, are in the open air. Baseball's Blue Jays share this facility with the Toronto Argonauts football team. The stadium hosts events all year round.

Tourism

Many Museums

Tourists in Toronto are often drawn to the city's many museums. The Art Gallery of Ontario is a popular choice. It is the eighth largest art museum in North America. There are more than 25,000 works of art on display inside the gallery.

Many visitors to Toronto also tour the Royal Ontario Museum. It is one of the most visited museums in the world. This is not surprising, considering the museum's first-rate exhibits. It has one of the best collections of ancient Chinese art outside China. It also has fascinating collections relating to other artwork, archaeology, and life sciences.

The Royal Ontario Museum has exhibits that will interest the whole family.

For a more contemporary museum, the MZTV Museum of Television is a great place to visit. This museum follows the history of television and the impact it has had on society. Through hundreds of television sets, visitors can trace the advancements of this important entertainment technology.

Among the exhibits at the MZTV Museum of Television is the first commercially available television set, the 1930 Baird Televisor.

The CN Tower

The Canadian National Tower, known simply as the CN Tower, is the tallest freestanding tower in the world. It is 553.33 m high from base to tip. The CN Tower serves as a communications tower, carrying several transmission facilities. It was completed in 1976 and was immediately one of the biggest tourist draws in Toronto.

When the weather is clear, visitors to the CN Tower's observation deck can see all the way to Niagara Falls.

About 2 million people visit the tower every year. They take the elevator to the observation deck where they can see for 160 km on a clear day. They can also visit the world's biggest revolving restaurant located at the top of the tower.

Ontario Place

Toronto's Ontario Place is a great attraction for families to visit. It offers a water park, playground, and heart-stopping rides. It also has an Imax theatre, pedal boats, and musical shows.

Rides and Games

Paramount Canada's Wonderland is in Toronto. This amusement park is open every year from May through October. Visitors to the park can test their courage on one of the many wild rides. Cliffhanger, a ride that swings, rolls, and twists passengers, is sure to have thrill-seekers on the edges of their seats. The park boasts North America's widest variety of rides with more than sixty to choose from. For younger visitors, the Scooby-Doo Haunted Mansion and Hanna-Barbera Land are popular. Paramount Canada's Wonderland also offers entertaining shows and an enormous water park.

Another popular tourist attraction is the Canadian National Exhibition (CNE). The CNE has been held since 1879, when it began showcasing agricultural

The CNE offers a variety of midway rides that children and adults can enjoy.

and technical products. Today, the CNE presents exhibits and pavilions celebrating all sorts of themes and concepts. Tourists can get close to animals at the petting zoo or try their skills at one of the many game booths on the exhibition grounds.

Vortex, Canada's only suspended roller coaster, can be found at Paramount Canada's Wonderland.

Paramount Canada's Wonderland boasts North America's widest variety of rides.

Olden Days

Tourists with a love for history are sure to stop at the Black Creek Pioneer Village. This nineteenth-century community, which is located in northwest Toronto, has been fully restored. The shops and homes transport visitors back to the 1860s. Staff and tour guides dress in garments like the ones residents of the village would have worn long ago. Cabinet makers, blacksmiths, and other craftspeople demonstrate the trade secrets of the time. Tourists can explore history by visiting an old mill, water wheel, the community doctor's house, and a schoolhouse.

The Black Creek Pioneer Village has over thirty restored buildings for visitors to explore.

Hockey Hall of Fame

The first stop for many sports fans is the Hockey Hall of Fame. This downtown facility houses souvenirs, photographs, equipment, and jerseys that track the history of one of Canada's favourite sports—ice hockey. Superstars including Wayne Gretzky, Gordie Howe, Bobby Orr, and Maurice Richard have all been inducted into the Hockey Hall of Fame.

Architecture

Casa Loma

An enormous, fortified house stands on top of one of the few hills in Toronto. The house is called Casa Loma, and it looks like something out of a fairy tale. Financier Sir Henry Mill Pellatt had Casa Loma built for himself and his wife. The "castle" cost $3.5 million to build, and it took about three years to complete.

Casa Loma is perhaps the most elaborate house in the city. This structure has ninety-eight rooms, all of which reflect an **Edwardian** style. It also has marble floors and a grand staircase. Its amazing exterior design draws on the eighteenth-century **Gothic Revival** styles found in England. There are also **battlements** and secret passages throughout the grounds.

After Pellatt's businesses began to fail, he had to sell the castle. It is now operated as a tourist attraction.

Visitors to Casa Loma can tour the castle and stables or take in one of the many musical shows staged on the grounds.

City Hall

Toronto's "new" City Hall officially opened in September 1965. At that time, many people were amazed by its unique appearance. City Hall was designed by Viljo Revell and Associates out of Helsinki, Finland, and was built with the help of John B. Parkin Associates in Toronto.

City Hall is made up of two towers. The East Tower has twenty-seven floors and is 99.5 m high. The West Tower has twenty floors and is 79.4 m high. The two towers curve and face each other, giving the impression of a circle that was separated in the middle. To build the hall, 69,574 cubic m of concrete, 9,144 metric tonnes of reinforced steel, 8,732 sq m of plate glass, 161 km of piping, and 304,800 m of electrical wiring was used. City Hall's grounds also encompass Nathan Phillips Square and the Peace Garden.

The design of City Hall has won many architectural awards.

Queen's Park

Looking at the stately buildings of the Provincial Legislature, it is hard to imagine the heated debates that take place inside. The Legislature Building, called Queen's Park, was completed on College Street and University Avenue in 1896. The granite and pink sandstone used in the construction give the building a look of strength and dignity. The Victorian style in which it was built shows the British influence on the province and the country at the time. Visitors to Queen's Park can tour the building and admire the elaborate hardwood carvings and beautiful staircase in the lobby. A collection of Canadian art can be found throughout Queen's Park.

Amid the skyscrapers and modern architecture in downtown Toronto, Queen's Park is a welcome reminder of the past.

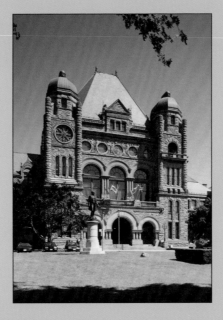

Fascinating Facts

1 The tallest office building in downtown Toronto is First Canadian Place. It stands seventy-two storeys high.

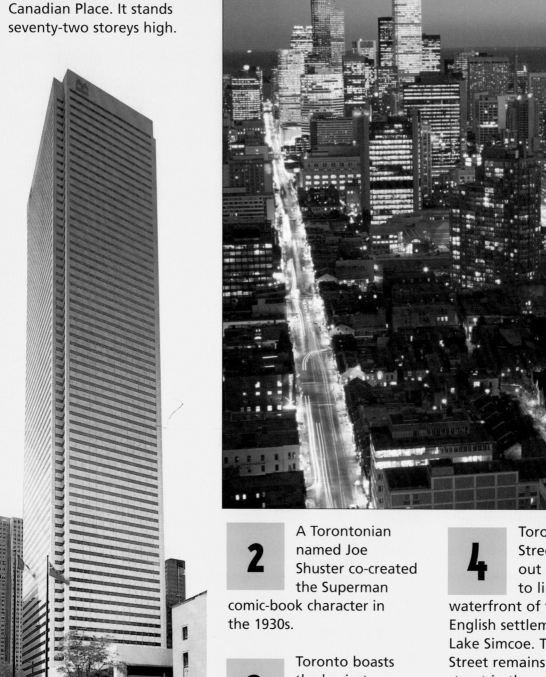

2 A Torontonian named Joe Shuster co-created the Superman comic-book character in the 1930s.

3 Toronto boasts the busiest library system in North America.

4 Toronto's Yonge Street started out as a trail to link the waterfront of the first English settlement with Lake Simcoe. Today, Yonge Street remains the longest street in the world. It is 1,896 km long.

5 While building the Skydome, workers found a cannon from the War of 1812, the gold handle from a cane, a 100-year-old mustard jar, and bottles from 1822 as they laid the foundations.

6 Sir Henry Mill Pellatt's extravagant home and its furnishings may have been his downfall. Shortly after Casa Loma was built, Pellatt had to auction his castle off for much less than it was worth because he could no longer afford it.

7 Television-watchers can see many Toronto landmarks on the Canadian programs *Kids of Degrassi*, *Degrassi Junior High*, and *Degrassi High*, which were all based in Toronto.

8 Toronto is a Huron word meaning "place of meeting."

9 In 1989, Toronto was awarded the title of "biggest garbage producer in the world."

10 In April 1904, a terrible fire spread through Toronto. The blaze lasted eight hours and spread from building to building. Firefighters came from Hamilton, Brantford, London, Peterborough, Niagara Falls, and even Buffalo, New York, to help put the fire out.

Activities

Based on what you have read try to answer the following questions.

Multiple Choice

1 The Blue Jays:

a) won the World Series four times during the 1980s and 1990s.

b) were the first non-American team to win the World Series.

c) folded after their 1993 World Series victory.

2 Toronto's climate is made less harsh because of:

a) the winds off Lake Ontario.

b) the New York weather system.

c) the large buildings downtown.

3 After the War of 1812:

a) York was destroyed and never rebuilt.

b) York was destroyed and rebuilt as Toronto.

c) York was destroyed and rebuilt.

4 Bay Street is:

a) the city's financial centre.

b) where fishing boats dock.

c) the host of the Street Festival.

5 Toronto is said to have

a) more Chinese people than Hong Kong.

b) more Irish people than Belfast.

c) more Italian people than Florence.

True or False.

6 William Lyon Mackenzie led a successful rebellion to take over the government.

7 Toronto's municipalities came together in 1998 to form the City of Toronto.

8 Uniformed police officers have patrolled Toronto since 1834.

9 Mel Lastman has served ten terms as the mayor of Toronto.

10 Casa Loma was built as a personal residence for a local financier.

Answers:
1. b); 2. a); 3. c); 4. a); 5. c). Answers: 6. False. His rebellion failed, but helped to make the British change the system. 7. True. 8. False. The officers did not have uniforms until 1837. 9. False. He was the mayor of North York for ten terms before becoming the mayor of Toronto. 10. True.

More Information

Books

Mackay, Claire and Johnny Wales. **The Toronto Story**.Toronto: Annick Press Ltd., 1990.

Mitchell, Scott. **Secret Toronto: The Unique Guidebook to Toronto's Hidden Sites, Sounds, and Tastes**. Oakville: ECW Press, 1998.

Murphy, Wendy and Jack. **Toronto**. New York: Blackbirch Press, 1992.

Prezeau, Nathalie. **Toronto: The Family-Tested Guide to Fun Places**. Toronto: Word-of-Mouth Production, 1999.

Web sites

Casa Loma

http://www.casaloma.org

General Information about Toronto

http://www.toronto.com

http://www.afghan-network.net/Toronto

http://www.city.toronto.on.ca

http://www.torinfo.com

http://www.math.toronto.edu/toronto

Sports Teams

http://www.torontomapleleafs.com

http://www.nba.com/raptors

http://www.bluejays.com

Some Web sites stay current longer than others. To find information on Toronto, use your Internet search engine to look up such topics as "CN Tower," "Toronto Zoo," "Winterfest," or any other topic you want to research.

Glossary

amalgamated: combined

American Revolution: a conflict between thirteen British colonies in North America and Britain that lasted from 1775 to 1783

auxiliary: additional, extra

battlements: low, protective walls with gaps at intervals, originally used to fire weapons from

bootlegging: illegally making and selling alcohol

borough: a municipality smaller than a city

dismantled: taken apart, stripped down

Edwardian: relating to the styles that were popular during the reign of King Edward VII, from 1901 to 1910

Gothic Revival: renewal of a medieval building style which makes use of pointed towers, windows, and arches

improv: comedy done on-the-spot without scripts or preplanning

Loyalists: people who remained loyal to Britain during the American Revolution

representative government: a system of government based on elected representatives

retractable: able to be pulled back or inward

Sabbath: a religious day of rest; it is Sunday for Christians and Saturday for people of the Jewish faith

suburban: residential district lying outside the central part of a town

Index